THE
BLUE BIRD WISH
COMES TRUE

When they are in
the ninth grade,
they join Horizon
Club.

When they are ten
or in the fifth grade,
they "fly up" to be-
come Camp Fire Girls.

Blue Birds are the
seven-, eight-, and
nine-year-old members.

All these girls belong to
CAMP FIRE GIRLS, INC.
16 East 48th Street
New York 17, New York

a national youth organization for girls seven
or in the second grade through high school

DEAR PARENTS:

THE BLUE BIRD WISH COMES TRUE is planned to help your daughter explore new ways with people, places, materials, ideas. Most of the activities are for her to do at home, some with your help, of course. You and she can read the book together, or she can read some of it herself.

Here are some facts about Blue Birds:

1. Blue Birds are members of Camp Fire Girls, Inc., 16 East 48th Street, New York 17, N. Y.

2. The Objectives of the organization are to encourage in every girl through an educational-recreational program:

> the application of her religious, spiritual, and ethical teachings to her daily living; a love of home and family that grows as she grows; pride in woman's traditional qualities—tenderness, affection, and skill in human relationships; deep love of her country, the practice of democracy, readiness to serve; the capacity for fun, friendship, and happy group relations; the formation of healthful habits; the ability to take care of herself, to do her work skillfully, and to take pleasure in it; interests and hobbies she can enjoy with others, and alone; love of the out-of-doors and skill in outdoor living; a happy heart that will help her find beauty, romance, and adventure in the common things of daily life.

The Blue Bird program helps girls develop through a variety of constructive experiences such as music, games, handcraft, dramatic play, homecraft, trips into the community, and guided social relationships within the group.

3. Girls of all races and creeds belong to Camp Fire Girls. They may become Blue Birds when they are seven years old or in the second grade. They "fly up" into the Camp Fire division when they are ten years old or in the fifth grade. Later, they belong to Horizon Club, for girls in ninth grade through high school. Girls may join at any age from seven to eighteen.

4. The groups usually meet once a week in homes, schools, churches, synagogues, or community centers. Each Blue Bird group has up to twenty members.

5. There is a registered leader and often an assistant leader with each group. The volunteer leaders receive training and guidance from the local and national Camp Fire Girls organization. Each group must have one, but not more than five sponsors. These may be parents or individuals designated by an organization to serve as group sponsors.

6. The cost of being a Blue Bird is very small. National dues for each member are $1.00 a year. The costume may be bought a piece at a time. Group expenses are small and are often met by group money-earning activities.

7. The Camp Fire Girls program in each community is made possible by the devoted work of volunteers, many of them your neighbors and friends, as well as by financial support from the community usually from the Community Chest or United Fund.

The name "Blue Bird" comes from Maeterlinck's play, *The Bluebird*, which has been freely rewritten for children on pages 18-22. The play tells of two children who look all over the world for the Bluebird of Happiness and find that it was at home all the time.

We hope that you and your daughter will enjoy becoming part of the Camp Fire Girls family, and that this book will help you spend some happy hours together.

Cordially,

Martha F. Allen
National Director
Camp Fire Girls, Inc.

3

How Blue Birds Came To Be

ONCE UPON A TIME there were no Blue Birds or Camp Fire Girls. That was quite some time ago, 1910 to be exact. Then one day a man and his wife decided to do something about this. They had a family camp. Their children and the children of their friends spent many wonderful hours together.

Everyone had so much fun at the camp of Dr. and Mrs. Luther Halsey Gulick that the family agreed to have a camp just for girls. The name of the camp was Camp Sebago-Wohelo on a lake in Maine. The camp was one of the earliest for girls. Here girls swam, canoed, hiked, cooked out of doors, danced and sang.

Dr. Gulick thought that children learned while they played just as they did in school. A great many of his friends believed this too. Camp Fire Girls was formed so that girls could have fun with friends at home, at school and at camp.

In the beginning Camp Fire Girls was only for older girls, but in 1913 Blue Bird groups began to meet, and have been meeting ever since wherever girls like you and your friends want to make the Blue Bird Wish come true.

Dear Girls

This book tells about Blue Birds,
the junior group of Camp Fire Girls,
and all the fun they have.

It shows many ways you can have fun, learn new
things, and help other people.

Some things are to do by yourself or
with a friend.

Some things are for you to do with a grownup
at home.

And some things are for you to do in your
Blue Bird meetings.

EDITH SUNLEY

THIS BOOK was written by Edith Sunley,
formerly Division of Program Services, Camp Fire Girls, Inc.
The pictures were drawn by Marg. Hartelius, artist.

What's In This Book

Hi!   My name is Betty Blue Bird.
I have lots of fun with my friends in
Blue Birds, and you can, too.

7

Jane Visits A Blue Bird Meeting

Betty Blue Bird has a special friend named Jane.

Jane says, "What do you do in Blue Birds? Could I be a Blue Bird, too?"

Betty Blue Bird tells her, "Come to a meeting with me. You'll find out!

We have meetings once a week after school.

Blue Birds are like a club."

Jane asks, "Who is that?"

"Oh, that's our leader," says Betty Blue Bird.

"She is Barbara's mother.

My mother helps sometimes."

8

"Hello, Jane!" says a
Blue Bird. "Have something
to drink.
I am hostess today."

"What will we do in Blue Birds
this time?"
"Let's talk it over," says the
leader.
"There are lots of things
we can do."

Usually Blue Birds sing or
play a game at every meeting.
They like to say the Blue Bird
Wish together.

"The Blue Bird Wish!" Jane asks. "What's that?"

9

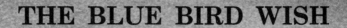

THE BLUE BIRD WISH

To have fun

To learn to make beautiful things

To remember to finish what I begin

To want to keep my temper most of the time

To go to interesting places

To know about trees and flowers and birds

To make friends

"Here is the Blue Bird Wish,"
says Betty Blue Bird to Jane,
"and Blue Birds do lots of things
to make it come true."

A WISH COMES TRUE

What will we do in Blue Birds?

Come on! I'll show you!

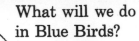

To have fun

They're telling what they like to do.

That's one way we have fun.

Those are cute!

11

To learn to make beautiful things

Sometimes we paint
or work with clay.

or cook

or make presents

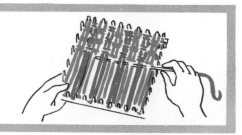

or help things grow

or sing songs we like.

What do you think she
remembered?

To want to keep my temper most of the time

Oh! They
forgot!

But they
try hard.

13

To meet new people, like

telephone operators,

policemen and firemen,

people who work in stores,

and people who make things.

To see new things, like taking

short trips on buses

and trains and boats

and even planes

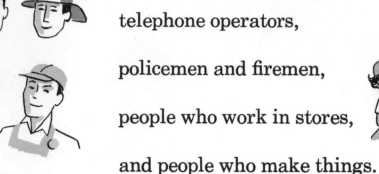

Or visiting the zoo

Or a farm

What interesting places would you like to see?

"Wait for me!"   "I wonder if they know about me!"

To make friends

There's room for you in Blue Birds too.

15

HOW
JANE BECAME
A BLUE BIRD

I talked to the
leader today.

Sounds like
a good idea
for my girl!

Oh, I want to
be a Blue Bird!

 CAMP FIRE GIRLS, INC.
MEMBERSHIP CARD

NAME

CITY

REGISTERED AS:

Marila J. Allen
NATIONAL DIRECTOR

She paid a dollar
to belong.
The leader gave
her the member-
ship card.

Later she got her Blue Bird pin
Only members can wear them.

For her birthday
her parents gave her
a real surprise.

At her first meeting, the Blue Birds told her about their rules.

Our Blue Bird Meetings

Be on time so we can get started.

Help get things ready.

Listen to other girls' ideas.

Tell your own ideas.

Help put things away.

Try to help everybody have a good time at the meeting.

"You have to learn our rules," the girls told Jane.
"We made them up ourselves for our meetings."
"We help each other remember."

"And now," said the leader, "does anyone know how Blue Birds got their name?"
Not one Blue Bird knew.
"Would you like me to tell you?" she said.

17

How Blue Birds Got Their Name

ONCE UPON A TIME, not as long ago and far away as you might think, lived a sister and brother named Mytyl and Tyltyl. They lived in a tiny cottage at the edge of the forest with their father and mother, who were very poor.

Mytyl and Tyltyl helped all they could at home.

One night after they had been tucked into bed, the door of their room opened slowly, and in hobbled a little old woman. She was lame and bent over, and had a patch over one eye, but her smile was warm and friendly.

"Who are you?" asked the children. They never guessed she was really a good fairy.

18

"My name is Berylune, and I am looking for the bluebird. My little girl is sick and, to get well, she must be happy. Only the bluebird will bring her happiness."

"We have a bird. See, he's over there in the cage," said Mytyl.

"But he isn't a bluebird," Tyltyl quickly added. "And anyway, he's *our* bird!"

Berylune put on her glasses and looked at Tyltyl and then at the little bird. "I see," she said. "Will you help me find the real bluebird, the Bluebird of Happiness, so that my little girl can laugh and run and play?" she asked.

"Oh, we will, we will! How do we begin looking for it?"

The old woman smiled and said,

> "Just hear what you can hear,
> And see what you can see,
> Try what you can try,
> And think what it might be."

"Oh, that would be fun!" they told her. "We're so tired of having nothing interesting to do at home!"

They put on their clothes and ran out. They didn't hear her say, "But wait! The Bluebird of Happiness might be very close."

What strange and wonderful adventures they had! First they came to the Land of Beautiful Things, where dwelled all living creatures, many lovely trees and birds and flowers. But no real bluebird.

Then they came to the Land of Remembering, where they were greeted kindly by three smiling girls named Help Others, Good Temper, and Try Hard. But no real bluebird. And last they came to the Land of Fun, where they made new friends, met old friends, and all played and worked together. But no real bluebird. For at each place, when they asked for the bluebird, they had the same answer:

"Just hear what you can hear

And see what you can see.

Try what you can try,

And think what it might be."

"To find the Bluebird will take longer still.

Look over the meadow and around the hill."

The longer they looked, the farther they went, until they found themselves right back where they had started, in their own back yard.

"We're home! We're home! Everything looks wonderful!" And how they hugged their father and kissed their mother!

Just then a bird sang.

"Do you hear what I hear?" said Mytyl.

"Do you see what I see?" said Tyltyl.

It was their own little bird hopping in his cage, and now they could see that it was blue!

"Do you suppose *that* could be the Bluebird of Happiness?" they shouted.

They decided to try and find out if it really was the Bluebird. So they took their bird to visit the sick little girl. She was lying on her bed, pale and sad. As soon as she saw the bird, she smiled happily and jumped out of bed. Then they knew.

"The Bluebird! Yes, it must be the Bluebird of Happiness! And it was at home all the time!"

Just then the old woman came to them, smiling, and said, "Well, my dears, now you know better how to find the Bluebird of Happiness wherever you are, through love, thought and kindness, and how to bring it to other people.

"You heard what you could hear,

And saw what you could see,

You tried what you could try,

And saw what it might be."

And now *you* know how Blue Birds got their name, because they are happy and make other people happy with the things right around them.

Adapted from *The Children's Blue Bird* by Georgette Le Blanc with permission of Dodd Mead & Co.

Would you like to make
the Blue Bird Wish
come true for you?

Just turn the page and begin.

Making Beautiful Things

Blue Birds wish "to learn to make beautiful things."

Here are some ideas for you to try at home.

Ask your mother to help you get ready to work.

Buttermilk And Chalk Drawing

Have you ever drawn with colored chalk?

You know how pretty the colors are, but they smudge your hands and clothes.

If you use buttermilk with the chalk, the colors will be prettier than ever, but will stay on the paper and not on you.

This is what you will need

Colored
Chalk

A big piece of paper.
Colored paper is nice sometimes.

A small can
filled with buttermilk

There are two ways of working.

This is one way. You can spread the buttermilk on the paper with a spoon. Then draw on the wet paper with chalk.

Or you can dip the chalk into the buttermilk. Then draw on the paper with the wet chalk. Draw with two pieces at a time if you like!

Now, what will you draw?

A pretty design?

A picture of you doing something you like?

A picture of you doing something you have just learned how to do?

People or animals in a story you know?

Some place you have been?—boat yard, circuses, farm houses with trees or flowers.

Every Blue Bird makes a different picture!

Modeling With Sugar Dough

Here is an easy way to make your own modeling clay.

It is pretty and easy to use.

If you bake it until it is hard, you can eat it too. Are your hands clean to begin?

Now just add

1 cup of water with some vege-table color in it   and   2 cups of sugar

to

3 cups of flour

Mix everything together well in a big bowl.

Use your hands.

Now the sugar dough is ready to make into anything you can think of.

Pretty shapes

Animals

People

Puppet heads

Doll furniture

Table decorations

Tray favors

Sugar dough is a recipe—other recipes you might use are cornstarch and salt, sawdust and liquid starch.

Here are things you could find to decorate what you make.

From around the house

From outdoors

Crayon On Cloth

Have you ever used your crayons to make designs on cloth? Try it.

Then you can use the cloth to make a scarf or apron or mat. Cotton in a soft color is best.

Cut the edges of the cloth with pinking shears.

Fasten it down so it won't slide around.

Use thumbtacks or gummed tape.

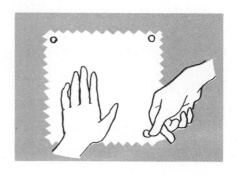

Draw something you have seen, zoo, water works, railroad station or library.

Draw something you like, people or animals or flowers or birds or butterflies or trees or the sky.

It can be all over or just on the border.

Fill in the colors very well.

Dampen another cloth and lay it over the drawing.

Press with a hot iron.

Now the color will stay in the drawing for a few washings.

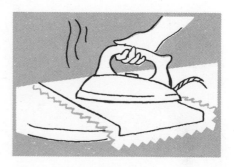

Make Believe

Play Places

You can make a private place to play in a corner of your room, or in the yard, garage, attic, or basement. Get a friend to help you.

An old blanket or sheet over a table.

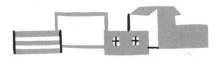

Big empty cartons for furniture. Wooden ones are good if you can get them.

A basket full of hats and jewelry and old clothes to dress up in.

A basket full of cans, dishes, boxes, dolls, clocks and other things good to pretend with.

If you ask, people may help you save things for your play place.

Try to keep everything together, so you and your friends can always find things.

Sometimes Blue Birds have a play place in their meeting room.

Paper Bag Puppets

Your puppet can be anyone you like, a man or animal or funny person or someone from a story.

Sometimes you won't know who it is until you have finished making it.

Take a brown paper bag with a square bottom.

Make a face on one side of the bag with crayons or paints.

The face should be big so that people can see it.

Stick your hand inside to make your puppet move.

You can paste things on to make eyes, eyebrows, noses, mouths and hair.

How about a hat for your puppet?

You may want to play with the puppet by yourself. Or you may want to give a show.

Betty Blue Bird Tells
Some Ideas
for a Good Puppet Show

1. A puppet should move when it talks. It should talk loudly.

2. A puppet should not move or talk when another puppet is talking. That way, everyone can hear who is talking.

3. Sometimes the puppet can say funny things to the audience. Or it can peep from under the curtain, if you have one.

4. The best fun is when you make up your own story. You can act out a fairy tale too. The puppets don't have to say the same thing every time.

Growing Up In Families

All kinds of people are in Blue Bird families.

Make a picture of your family and you.   Paste it here.

At Blue Bird meetings, girls like to do things for parents sometimes.

Parents like to visit the group sometimes, too.

Making presents

A party for mothers

Fathers at a picnic

Mothers helping at meetings

New Things To Try At Home

Polish on a soft rag.
Enough, but not too much!
Spread it thin, all over.
Rub hard, hard, harder.
Look how shiny!

You can't hear talking
when the vacuum roars.
But you can hear the prickly
sound of the dust,
Flying through the long hose.
You hold the hose in one place
till the prickly dust is gone.

Down push the needle, and
Down pull the thread.
Up push the needle, and
Up pull the thread.
In and out, along, along.
Tie a knot! It's done!

Ask Mother What You Can Learn To Do

Washing clothes is fun,
doll clothes or your own.

Lots of suds, lots of squeezing,
rinse up and down in cool clear
water, until no more suds.

Shake! Dribbly drops! Drip dry!

Irons are hot, hot, hot.

So fingers stay around the
cool, cool handle.

Push the point, push the point,

To every edge and corner,

Till all the wrinkles go.

"Hello!"

"I'm so glad to see you."

"Mother, this is Barbara."

"Please sit down."

"Won't you have some cake?"

"Do come again soon."

"Goodbye!"

Good To Eat

Blue Birds like to fix good food
for themselves and their friends.

Measuring Is Important

Here are spoons and cups to measure just right.
You make the foods come level with the top.

Setting the Table

See how everything
is in a row
at the bottom

Do you know ways of making a table look pretty?

Betty Blue Bird Tells
What Not To Forget To Remember.

1. Wash your hands CLEAN before you cook.

2. Be sure that a grownup is right there when you use the stove.

3. Stand on a stool, but NEVER on a chair.

4. Use thick pot holders to pick up hot spoons or hot pans.

5. If you need a sharp knife, ask a grownup to do the cutting.

6. If you spill something on the floor, wipe it up right away. If you don't, someone may slip and get hurt.

7. Wear short sleeves near the stove.

8. Shut the oven door so that no one will fall over it.

The cleanup committee

Snacks For Home Or Meeting

Banana Milk Shake

Mash a ripe banana in a bowl.
Do this with a fork.

Pour 1 cup of milk on the banana.
Beat with an egg beater.

Pour into two glasses.
This is a Banana Milk Shake for two.

Toast Specials

Cinnamon Mix

Mix together in a cup
  1 teaspoon cinnamon
  2 tablespoons sugar

Make two pieces of toast.

Butter it while hot.

Sprinkle it with mix.

Cut toast in strips.

Eat it while it's hot.

Raisin Peanut Butter

Mix in a small bowl
  ¼ cup peanut butter
  2 tablespoons seedless
    raisins chopped

Make two pieces of toast.

Spread it with mix.

Cut toast in strips.

Good!

Easy Pudding

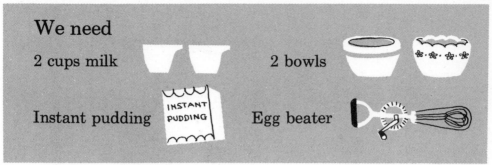

We need

2 cups milk

Instant pudding

2 bowls

Egg beater

Put two cups of milk in a bowl.

Then pour in the pudding mix.

Beat and beat with the egg beater.

Next pour it in a pretty bowl.

In five minutes it is ready to eat.

Sometimes you can add banana slices or nuts on top.

A Pretty Party Punch

Pile fruit halfway up a tall glass.

Fruit may be fresh or frozen.

Bananas and berries are good.

Fill the glass with fruit juice

   or lemonade.

Put a big scoop of sherbet on top.

Yummy!

All Outdoors

Ask some Blue Birds,
"What do you like to do best outdoors?"

They will tell you different things.

"Cooking out."

"Hiking to new places."

DEBBIE

"Singing around the fire."

SUSAN

"Playing games."

"Going to Camp."

LINDA

JUDY

KATHY

You can do many things outdoors with your friends and family, the way Blue Birds do.

Penny Hike

On a penny hike, you flip a penny, every time you come to a corner.
 If it is heads, you turn left.
  If it is tails, you turn right.
 Everyone takes turns flipping.
 You never know where you'll end up!
 Take a grownup so you won't get lost!

Trail Marking Hike

You need two teams, one to follow the other.

The first team goes ahead.
They mark a trail with
sticks, stones or grass.

The second team waits for
half an hour.
Then they follow the trail.

Turn
left

Go
this way

Turn
right

Watch Bird Hike

Everybody watches for a certain
thing on a hike.

At the end, each tells what she saw.

What you look for depends on where you are. For instance:
How many different trees do you see?
What jobs do you see people doing?
What signs of the season do you see?
How many kinds of things on wheels?

Cookouts

A good fire can be made with wood or with charcoal.

How Blue Birds Help At Cookouts

1. They gather dry sticks and twigs to start the fire.

   They know a twig is dry and dead if it makes a snapping noise when it's broken.

2. They help the grownup lay the fire.

   They light matches only when a grownup is there.

3. They help get the food ready.

4. They are watchmen to make sure that flying sparks don't set leaves or grass on fire.

5. They help gather paper and other rubbish that will burn.

6. They put into trash cans the things that won't burn.

7. They help make sure the fire is all put out with water or sand.

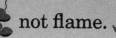

Toasting On A Stick

Choose a green stick for toasting things because a dead stick will catch on fire.

Let a grownup use the knife to cut and point the stick.

Always toast things over coals not flame.

How about toasting a s'more?

What Is A S'more?

You make it like a sandwich, only it's for dessert.

A graham cracker   Half a chocolate bar   A marshmallow you have toasted on a stick until it's golden brown.   Another graham cracker

These are so good they make you want some more. That's how they got their name!

Blue Birds Say, "Don't Be A Litterbug!"

Litterbugs drop things on the ground and out of cars.

Blue Birds remind people, "Use a trash can or a litter bag." You can decorate a litter bag made out of cloth or paper. Keep it in your car or take it on hikes and picnics. This helps Mother Nature keep her house clean for everybody!

AND

A wonderful part of the Blue Bird Wish is learning about trees and flowers and birds. The world is full of exciting things—in the sky, in the trees, on the ground,—everywhere!

There are clouds, wind, rain,
ice and snow to learn about
There are buds, blossoms, and
green and golden leaves to discover
There are big bugs, little bugs, bugs with
many legs and some with funny spots.

Living Things

"To know about trees and flowers and birds," says the Blue Bird Wish.

And about animals and babies and everything alive!

Blue Birds are friends to birds all the year around.

Springtime Nests

You can help the birds find things they can use to build nests.

Good things are pieces of grass or moss, also pieces of yarn, not more than three inches long.

Quiet colors are best, like gray, brown, dark green.

Put them in a tree or other place where the birds can find them.

Winter Feasts

In winter, birds have a hard time finding things to eat.

Well, one thing they like is raisins.

Raisins on a string!

Thread a big needle with heavy thread.

Push the needle through the raisins.

When you have a long string full of raisins, loop it over branches so that the birds can sit and peck the raisins off.

Another Treat For Birds Is Peanut Butter

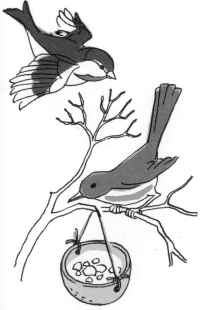

Take half of an empty grapefruit or orange rind.

Make two holes near the rim for a handle.

Run a piece of string through the holes and tie knots.

Fill the basket with peanut butter or suet.

Hang it on a tree.

Bird Baths For Warm Weather

When warm weather comes, people like
to drink a lot.

They like to cool off in a bath
or under the hose.

So do birds. But sometimes it is not easy
for them to find a drinking pool
or swimming pool.

You can make one and watch them enjoy it.

Take a shallow pan, or
an old salad bowl.

Put it on the ground.

Keep it filled with two or three
inches of *clean* water.

Sometimes shy birds will come if
water is dripping into the pool. Dad
could help you punch a small hole
in the bottom of an old pail or a
big tin can.

Hang the pail above the pool.

Fill the pail with water every day.

A shower bath for birds!

Pretty Leaf Prints To Make

Take a walk and find some pretty leaves. See how many shapes you can find.

You can put them in a **magazine** to hold them when you are **walking**. This girl has a **maple leaf**.

Put your leaf on a table, with the smooth side down.

Cover it with a piece of **white typing paper**.

Rub the paper lightly with a crayon.

Isn't it fun to see the **shape of the leaf** coming through on the paper?

Cut out your leaf prints.

Paste them on colored paper if you like.

You can use these prints

    To decorate your room

    To make place mats

    To make party invitations

    To make table decorations

    To make greeting cards.

Fun To Find Out

How Far Does The Wind Blow?

Send a balloon message and find out.

Buy a blown-up balloon at the ten-cent store or from a street balloon man.

Make sure it is filled with helium gas, which is very light and will float your balloon high above the tree tops.

Wait for a very windy day.

Tie two cards onto the string.

One card will be a postcard addressed to you.

On the other card, ask the person who finds the balloon to mail the postcard back to you, and tell you where she found the balloon.

Then you will know how far the wind can carry things!

Secret Writing

Would you like to send your friend a secret message?

Give her a piece of plain white paper.

She is the only one who will know that you have used invisible ink on it!

Here is what you will need to write.

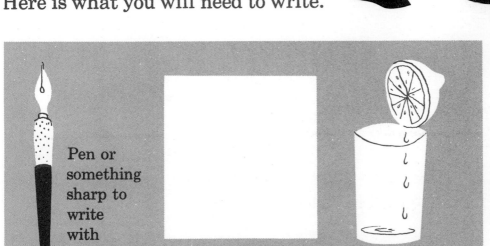

Pen or something sharp to write with

Typing paper

Lemon juice in a small glass

Write your message with the lemon juice. After it is dry, give it to your friend.

She holds the paper over something very hot, like an iron.

The heat will make the lemon juice turn brown so that she can read the message.

Making Your Own Telephone

Most girls love to talk on the telephone.

Here is a phone you and a friend can make.

You can use

2 paper drinking cups

or

2 clean ice cream cartons

or

2 tin cans (no sharp edges).

Punch a hole in the bottom of each one.

Then take 15 feet of strong cord.

Put each end of the cord into the cup and through the hole. Now tie a big button at each end of the cord to hold the cord in place.

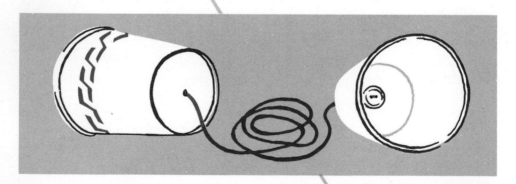

Now you and your friend both take a phone.

You take turns talking while the other person listens.

Hello! Can you hear me? Try it!

Games To Try

New Ways To Play Tag

Did you ever play in one of these ways?
Instead of running, everybody has to

tiptoe
or
walk

or hop on one foot

or hop on both feet.

And did you ever play this way?

When the person who is "It" is going to tag you, you can save yourself by doing one of these.

Statue tag	Wooden tag
Get into a pose and stay that way. "It" can stand and wait for you to move. If you move, "It" can tag you.	Touch something made of wood, like a tree or house. You can do this only three times before you can be caught. You can't touch the same thing twice.

Guess What

Do you know how to play
Run, Sheep, Run?
Streets and Alleys?
Towns or Cities?
Handkerchief Relay?
Ask your leader how to play them.
You might like to play "What Am I?"

It goes like this:

One girl leaves the room and the rest of you decide what animal she should be. When you have all agreed she may come back into the room and try to guess the animal. She may ask each girl in turn questions such as, "Do I have a short tail?" "Are my ears long and floppy?" The only answers the girls may give are "Yes" or "No." No hints, please. When she finally guesses what she is, the girl whose answer helped leaves the room. All of you should have a turn guessing whether you are a horse, a kangaroo or a bear.

Jump Rope Rhymes

Here is one Jump Rope Rhyme.

I asked my mother for fifteen cents
To watch the elephant jump the fence.
He jumped so high that he touched the sky
And never came back till the Fourth of July.

Hot Or Cold

Whoever is "It" leaves the room.

While she is gone, the others choose something in the room for her to guess, such as someone's shoe.

When she comes back, she points to different things in the room.

If she is far away from the right thing, everyone says "Cold," or "Very cold."

As she gets close to the right thing, they say "Warmer," or "Warm."

When she guesses it, she is "Hot" and someone else becomes "It."

The Silly Game

In this game, you mustn't laugh, no matter how silly something sounds.

The person who is "It" asks you different questions, like "What did you have for breakfast?" or "What did you see on TV last night?"

No matter what she asks, you must always say, "Boula Boula's Big Fat Toe" (or make up something else silly to say every time).

The first person who laughs becomes "It."

Don't you know other games you would like to play?

These can be Running games—Jumping games
    Games with a ball or Just a quiet talking game.

Games For The Whole Family

 Here are good games to try on your father or mother, or your brother or sister.

Play them at the table, or in the car, or any place.

Riddle-de-Dee

If you are "It," you decide to be a certain person or animal or thing, but you don't tell anyone what you are.

Say "Riddle-de-Dee, you can't guess me!"

Then tell a little bit about your new self.

If no one guesses, tell more until they do guess.

One Blue Bird said, "I have four legs. You put clothes inside me. I am made of wood."

You know what she was?

A chest of drawers!

The Mentioning Game

Everyone decides on a certain place they all know, like another room.

Then they take turns mentioning what is in the place.

Everyone mentions something different, like "Forks," or "Chairs," or "Curtains."

When no one can remember anything more, choose a different place.

Learning About Babies

Babies are full of life!

Blue Birds have fun playing with babies, and helping to look after them.

One good way to learn more about babies is to ask your mother about when you were very little.

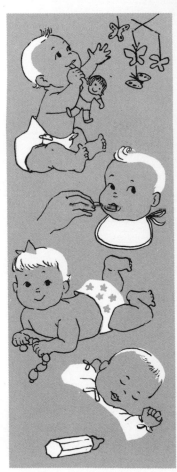

1. What were the first words you said?

2. How old were you when you started to walk alone?

3. What did you like doing most when you played by yourself?

4. What did you like best when your Daddy played with you?

5. Who was your first best friend?

6. What made you laugh? What made you cry?

7. Did you like taking a bath?

8. What was your favorite food?

9. What was the special thing that helped you go to sleep?

10. What were some of the cute things you did?

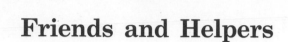

Friends and Helpers

Blue Birds like to make new friends and do nice things for people they know.

Talk over with your mother or leader how you could do something nice for one of these people near you.

A Neighbor

A Teacher

Blue Bird Leader

Your Family

Doing friendly things with other children is a special part of being a Blue Bird.

Sometimes they play together, or invite each other over, or send each other letters or presents.

Look around at the children you know, and think what friendly thing you can do.

Small Children

New Children

Sick Children

Another Blue Bird Group

When You Have A Friend Who Is Sick

Sometimes one of your friends gets sick and can't come to school or to Blue Bird meeting.

You know what it is like when you have to stay in bed and can't get up to play.

You can send her a card or letter, or call her up.

Here are some things to bring her to use while she is getting better.

1. Some play dough in a plastic bag. See Page 26. (Her mother can cover the bed with an old sheet while she plays.)

2. Old magazines to cut out and some paste.

3. A puppet to play with. See Page 30.

4. Some records or books to borrow.

5. Some leaves to make crayon leaf prints. See Page 47.

6. Some paper dolls you draw for her. She can cut them out.

> **What else can you think of?**

You Can Make
A Bouncing Ball On A String

Some children can't play ball because they can't run very well or can't see very well or have to stay in bed.

Here is a ball they can play with because it has a string on it to pull it back.

The string can be tied down while they play.

1. Take a hollow rubber ball.

2. Poke one small hole in one side with a metal knitting needle or a dull knife.

3. Take a very long shoelace and tie a double knot just above one of the metal tips.

4. Poke the knot through the hole with the eraser end of a pencil. Ask a grownup to help if it is hard to do.

5. Try using the ball. If the string is too short, make it longer by tying on another shoelace.

You can send this ball to
      A child you know who needs it
      or to a children's hospital near you
      or to
            Handicapped Children
            American Friends Service Committee
            20 South 12th Street
            Philadelphia 7, Pennsylvania

Music Makers

Can you make music without singing?

Anyone can play a glass-o-phone!

A Glass-o-Phone

Here's all you do.

Just take eight drinking glasses the same size.

Fill them with water.

Put more in some glasses than in others.

Now take a knife.

Tap the rim of each glass softly with the knife. Music!

Do you get different sounds from different glasses? Why?

Make up your own tunes and play a solo!

Do you know how to sing "Looby Loo?"

A Humbuzzer Band

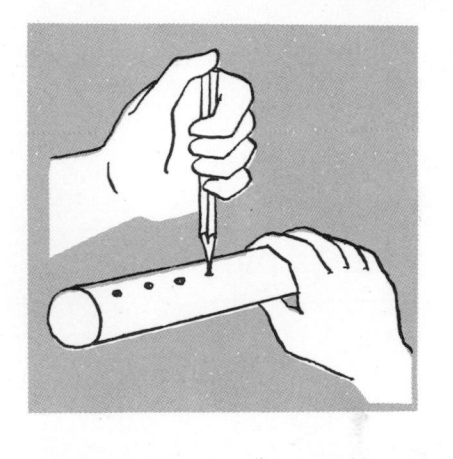

Take a big cardboard tube, like the one from paper towels.

Make it ten inches long.

Punch a row of four or five holes with scissors.

Turn a pencil in the holes until they are round.

Now cut a piece of wax paper the right size to fit over the end of the tube.

Fasten it with a rubber band.

Let's make music!

Hum into the open end.

Try different tunes,
some loud, some soft.

Put your fingers over
and off the holes.

Do you know "Sing Blue Birds Sing"?

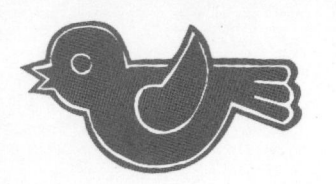

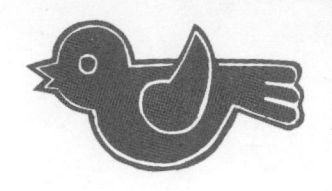

The Blue Bird Wish Song

Music by Mary Bolling Brown.

Learn this song with your family.

Some Blue Birds can play the piano part.

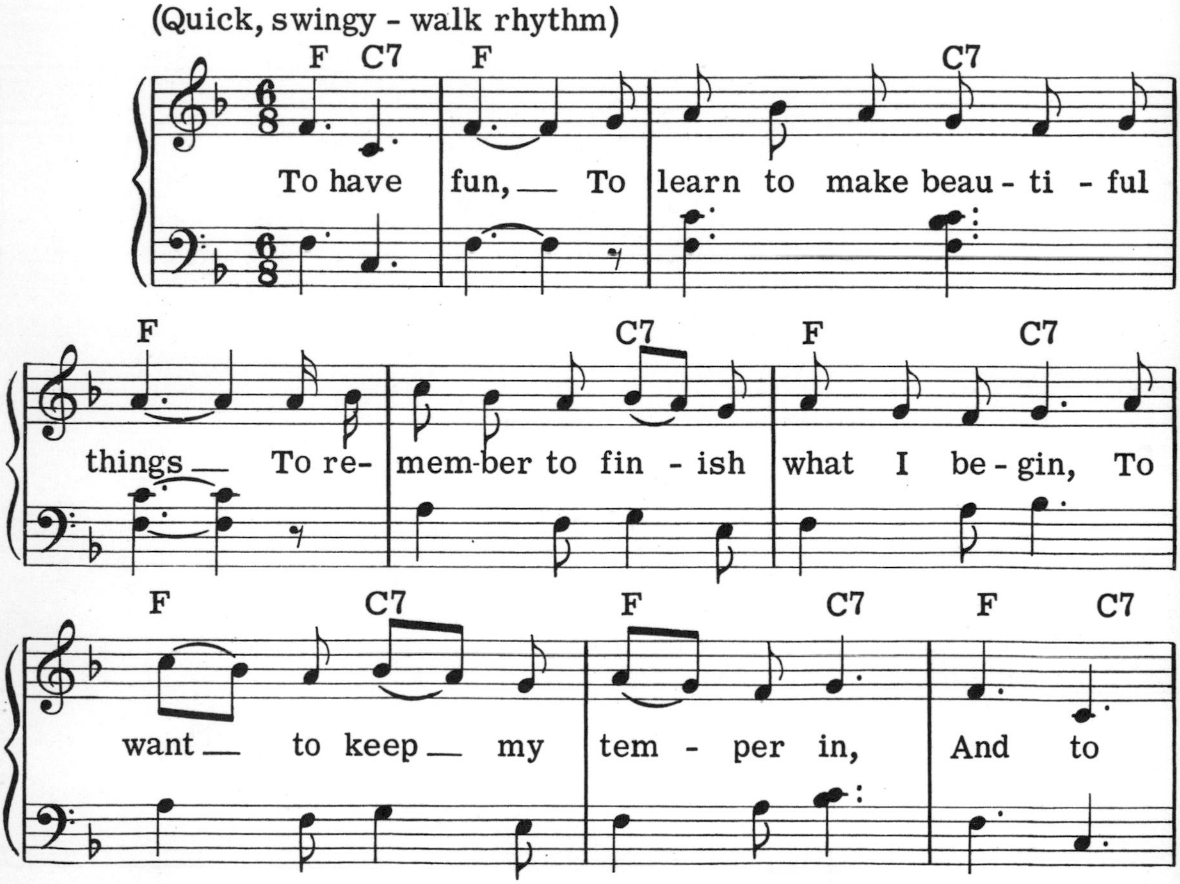
(Quick, swingy - walk rhythm)
F C7 F C7
To have fun, — To learn to make beau - ti - ful
F C7 F C7
things — To re- mem-ber to fin - ish what I be - gin, To
F C7 F C7 F C7
want — to keep — my tem - per in, And to

go _____ to | ev' - ry in-t'rest-ing | place, _____ to

learn _ a-bout _ the | beau-ti-ful trees, The | flow-ers, the birds _ and

things _____ like these, | And make | friends. _____

NOW
I AM A
CAMP FIRE
GIRL

Since the beginning of Blue Birds you knew you had something wonderful to look forward to—being a Camp Fire Girl. How much you have admired them when they helped the group learn new songs and games, or told about their meetings. They were such fun, but at the same time helpful and grown-up.

You are now ready to become a Camp Fire Girl. For some time now the group has been learning about honor beads, rank, symbolism and the Seven Crafts. You have also talked about the special way you will "fly up" into Camp Fire. You've learned the meaning of a new word, "ceremonial." A Fly-up Ceremonial is a little like graduation. It is a time when you are very serious and very happy. Something important is happening. *You* are growing up.

Your parents and the guests who attend the Fly-up Ceremonial will be proud with you. Your big sister Camp Fire Girl will open the door to an exciting new world when she puts on your red tie and says:

"Worship God — Seek Beauty — Give Service
Pursue Knowledge — Be Trustworthy — Hold on to Health
Glorify Work — Be Happy.

Wohelo and welcome. Wohelo means work, health, love. We hope you will be happy in the Law of Camp Fire Girls, as a Camp Fire Girl and one day when you reach the ninth grade, as a member of a Horizon Club."

ACKNOWLEDGMENTS

Miss Helen Ferris, *Junior Literary Guild*

Miss Josette Frank, *Child Study Association of America*

Miss Nancy Larrick, *Random House*

Dr. Irving Lorge, *Columbia University*

Acknowledgment is made to the above for their review of the manuscript in preparation.